Natalie,
"Success lies not [in doing your]
best, but in doing [...]"

Love,
Aunt Joyce & Uncle Gerry
5/28/11

Seek Happiness

copyright © 2008 Fountain Publishing

Published and printed in the U.S.A. by
Fountain Publishing
P.O. Box 80011, Rochester, MI 48306
www.fountainpublishing.com

Book and cover design by Karin A. Childs.

ISBN 10: 0-9748423-9-7
ISBN 13: 978-0-9748423-9-4

All rights reserved. No part of this publication may be reproduced or transmitted in any form or by any means, electronic or mechanical, including photocopying, recording, or any information storage or retrieval system, without prior permission from the publisher.

Seek Happiness

Words of Inspiration from Helen Keller

Edited and with photographs by Karin Alfelt Childs

🌿 Introduction 🌿

When a person who overcomes so much to triumph greatly speaks words of wisdom, they are worth listening to; for it is not words alone, but the source and origin of the words that determine their ultimate meaning and impact on the reader.

Helen Keller, blind, deaf, and mute, sought and found great happiness and fulfillment in her life. Notably, she also gave a great deal of happiness to others. These remarkable facts cannot help but inspire us all. She overcame the handicaps of the loss of two of our most critical senses, and the attendant faculty of communication through speech, all of which we normally regard as necessary to survival and happiness. That she then went on to lead a productive, creative, and serviceable life of immense achievement forces us to recognize that our own happiness is something for which we have ultimate responsibility. Any deficiency of happiness we experience can very rarely be blamed on anyone or anything else. Surely, this is one of the great meanings of her life for humanity and, therefore, we have chosen her quoted words "Seek Happiness" as the title of this book of wisdom gems. Helen Keller believed strongly in the power of the human spirit, no matter what the outer circumstances around it.

Happiness

has very little to do with outward circumstance.

The marvelous richness of human experience
would lose something of rewarding joy
if there were no limitations to overcome.

In every limitation we
overcome, and in the
higher ideals we thus
attain, the whole kingdom
of love and wisdom
is present.

If those who seek happiness would only stop one little minute and think, they would see that the delights they really experience are as countless as the blades of grass at their feet

or the drops of dew sparkling upon the morning flowers.

The altar is holy only when it represents the altar of our heart, upon which we offer the only sacrifices ever commanded—the love that is stronger than hate, and the faith that overcomes doubt.

*We please God better with useful deeds
than with many prayers or pious resignations.*

Love, the all-important doctrine, is not a vague, aimless emotion but the desire for good united with wisdom, and fulfilled in right action.

In our service to others, love is made visible.

Love provides the delicacy of perception to see wonders

in what before seemed dull and trivial.

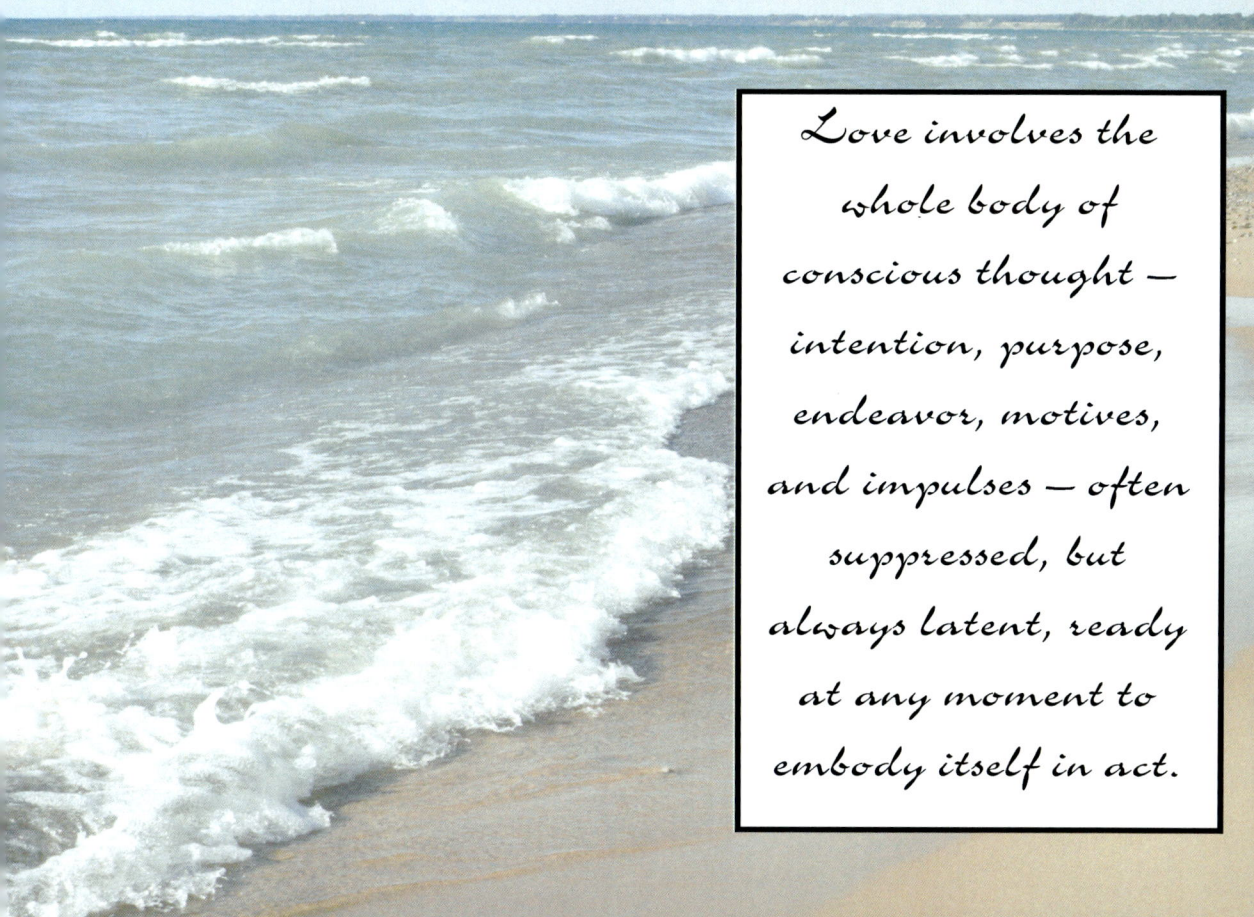

Love involves the whole body of conscious thought — intention, purpose, endeavor, motives, and impulses — often suppressed, but always latent, ready at any moment to embody itself in act.

I have never believed that my limitations were in any sense punishments or accidents.

If I had held such a view, I could never have exerted the strength to overcome them.

We can decide to let our trials crush us, or we can convert them to new forces of good.

. . . I believe that God is in me as the sun is in the color and fragrance of a flower—

the Light in my darkness, the Voice in my silence.

*Sick or well,
blind or seeing,
bound or free,
we are here
for a purpose.*

We may help ourselves to all the beauty of the universe that we can hold.

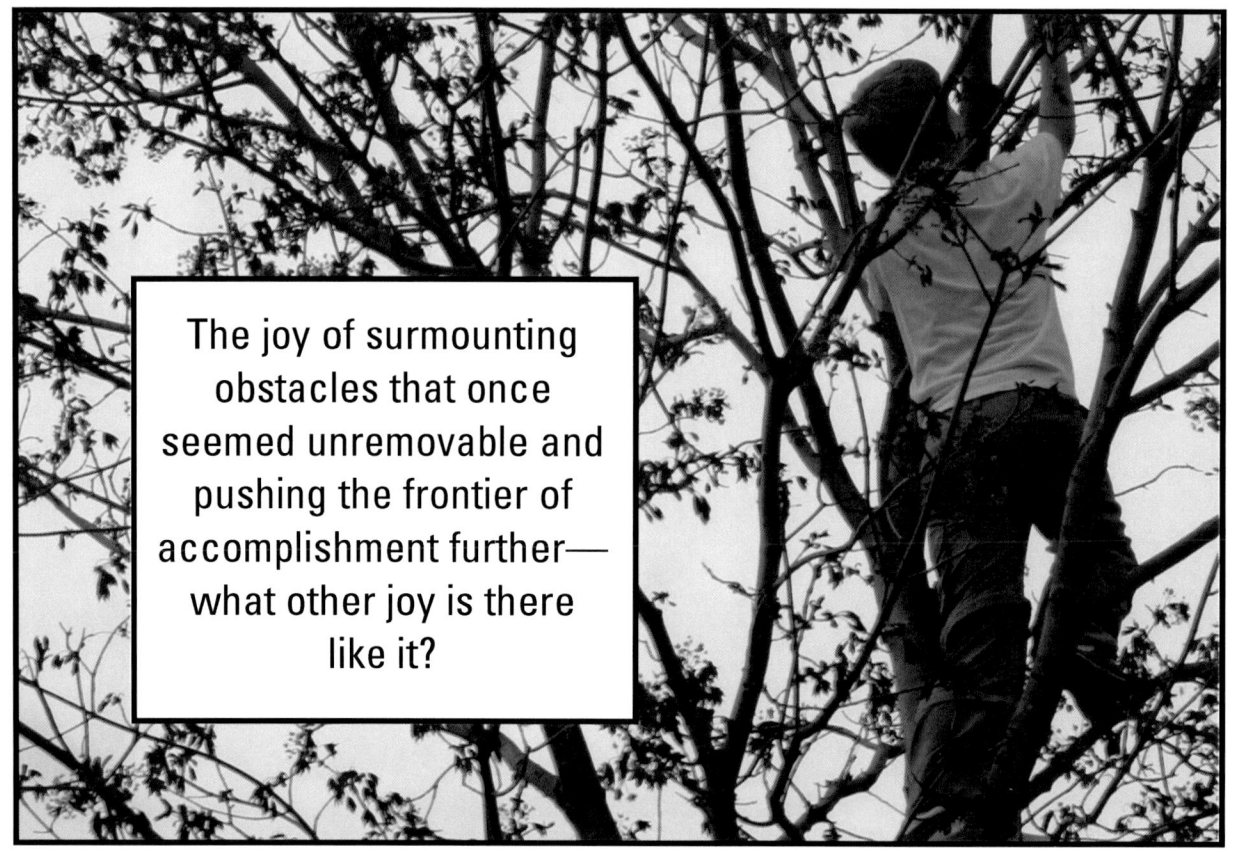

Only by striving
for what is beyond us
will we win
expansion and joy.

I believe that when the eyes within my physical eyes open upon the world to come, I will be consciously living in the country of my heart.

...heaven is not beyond us,

but
within us.

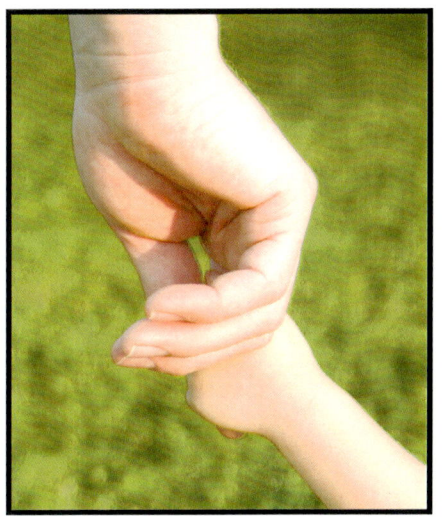

A simple, childlike faith in a Divine Friend solves all the problems that come to us upon this earth.

*We have nothing to do with
our birth into existence...*

*our birth into life
is a matter of
choice.*

Quotations taken from:

Light in My Darkness

by Helen Keller
Published by the Swedenborg Foundation, Inc.
www.swedenborg.com

A revised edition of
My Religion by Helen Keller,
Published 1927 by Doubleday & Co.
Republished 1960 by Swedenborg Foundation.

Also about Helen Keller: ***Shining Soul*** (DVD)
www.swedenborg.com

Notecards with quotes by Helen Keller are available at
www.fountainpublishing.com.

Other gift books:

Seeds: Infinite Possibilities, text by Emanuel
Swedenborg, photos by Karin A. Childs.
www.fountainpublishing.com